Land of Fire and Snow~ Hawaii's Big Island

by Scott C.S. Stone

ISLAND HERITAGE

For Lindley and Matthew,
Na keiki o ka aina

Published by
Island Heritage Limited
Leeside Taylors Road
Norfolk Island 2899
Australia

Produced in association with
Honolulu Publishing Company, Ltd.
36 Merchant Street
Honolulu, Hawaii 96813

FIRST EDITION
Copyright © 1983 Island Heritage Limited
ALL RIGHTS RESERVED

Please address orders, editorial correspondence and
catalog requests to our United States office:
Island Heritage Limited
550 North Nimitz Highway
Honolulu, Hawaii 96817
Phone (808) 526-1126

Printed and bound in Hong Kong
Library of Congress Catalog number 83-12843
ISBN 0-89610-091-X

...an island of fire and snow, coming out of the sea at the end of an epic voyage, rich in promise and cloaked in beauty and mystery; an island of dreams...

A Note at the Beginning

This book is intended for visitors and residents alike, in hopes each will find something evocative of this most spectacular island in the Hawaiian Archipelago. For convenience the book is sectioned: A brief history and overview is followed by a narrative look at each district of this highly diverse island, including an informal guide. The brevity of this book requires great condensation of a very large and interesting topic. The book may serve as a starting point for anyone with a greater curiosity who cares to investigate any of the fine Hawaii histories that are available.

Hawaii island is referred to as the "Big Island" for obvious reasons; it could just as easily have been called the "Orchid Island," or the "Volcano Isle." It is an island rich in culture, heritage and commerce; its people enjoy a lifestyle that garners the best offerings from its various races. Each person who visits finds here what he has already been carrying in his heart, and so it is an island for adventurers, for lovers, for scientists, for escapists, and for those who want to lie in the sun and do nothing at all.

The author is a once and future resident of the Big Island, and subject to all the biases and prejudices a writer can feel when he cares deeply about his home. No apologies are possible here; when an island weaves its enchantment and you are irretrievably under its spell there is nothing for it but to surrender. Perhaps the reader will surrender as well, and lose himself to an island that long ago drew explorers from far beyond the edge of the sea.

In the Wake of the Long Canoes

Out of antiquity and out of Asia an energetic race turned south and east and set out on voyages of discovery and colonization, crossing uncharted seas under strange new constellations. In great, double-hulled canoes superbly designed to ply the long swells of the Pacific, the voyagers aimed at something beyond the horizon, something that drew them onward, magnetizing their aspirations and their dreams.

In the sea they had found their food and recreation. There was a rhythmic echo between the coursing of their blood and the pull of the tides, and with deliberation they turned the prows of their canoes toward the unknown.

When they reached the apex of the great Polynesian triangle defined by the Society Islands, New Zealand and Hawaii, they were as far north as they would go, and they halted on an enormous island content that it would provide all they would need.

In all likelihood they came ashore on its southernmost point, staring in awe at the massifs that rose before them. Then, or soon, they would be awed by two other elements of nature—the eruptions of volcanoes and the fall of snow. They were not deterred by nature or by internecine conflicts, and so they founded an island kingdom.

For a millennium or more the Polynesians lived in splendid isolation: Subtle changes evolved into a new culture for this people whose love of the sea became matched by a love for the land. In their breasts burned the devotion to their place that is known to such a depth only by islanders. Chiefs rose and fell, men prospered, or died in cruel combat; a folklore developed. Laws, rules and customs spread islandwide and were accepted. The Polynesians had become Hawaiians.

Throughout the centuries the major Islands of the archipelago were populated and came under the control of kings or great chieftains. While there was diversity, the Islands were linked by the homogeneity of their people and culture, and if they were not yet a nation, they

Above, the vigor of an island race is illuminated by its high-spirited dances. Opposite page, intelligence and adaptability were characteristics of the Polynesians, whose epic voyages earned the continuing admiration of later seamen.

A portrait of King Kamehameha I by a contemporary artist.

were an entity, a society. It was at this moment that strangers arrived, shattering the veil of isolation and changing the course of Hawaiian history forever.

Captain James Cook—an explorer, cartographer, and navigator already famous for his discoveries—was changed, too, by his discovery of Hawaii for the Western world. In tragic confrontations, native Hawaiians were inflicted with venereal diseases, guns were introduced to ambitious chiefs, Cook was killed, and Hawaii was jerked rudely and permanently into the modern world. It was the beginning of the 19th century, and changes were coming at an accelerated pace to the Islands.

The largest island in the archipelago, Hawaii, gave its name to the entire chain of islands, and also produced the Islands' first and most memorable leader in Kamehameha I. Born in the Kohala section, this vigorous and ruthless man proved to be a remarkable leader. For all his employment of the *haoles*, the white strangers, and his quick adaptability to modern warfare and tactics, Kamehameha feared a too-quick modernization of the Islands and fought to keep the old ways, especially the *kapus*. The *kapu* system rigidly defined religious and social practices and held the Islands in a grip of traditional behavior and practices. Kamehameha died on the west coast of Hawaii island in

Engrossed in the sweet smell of the soil, a Hamakua farmer is surrounded by quiet beauty.

Opposite page, other vistas stretch before travelers who explore the island's far corners.

1819; though his dynasty continued, the *kapus* were broken and Hawaiians emerged from their customary and ritualistic past into an era ready for new ideas.

The new ideas were manifested in two powerful invasions: Bawdy, brawling whaling men, whose ships chased whales across thousands of miles in years-long voyages, put into Hawaii ports for resupply and recreation; and God-fearing missionaries who, in their own way, were as iron-willed as the whalers, settled in the Islands. Both groups astonished the native Hawaiians and caused almost equal controversy. The whalers regarded Hawaii as their personal playground, an easy place for women, whiskey and unwinding from the rigors of hard voyages. The missionaries regarded Hawaii as a fertile field for God's work, the natives as pagans who had an urgent need to be converted and the whaling men as devils incarnate. In time the whaling influence would pass, diminished by the production of petroleum which lessened the demand for whale oil.

The Civil War also took its toll on the ships, and in 1871 the Arctic ice caught and crushed 33 ships of the American whaling fleet. The industry never recovered. The missionaries extended their influence but their rigidity became somewhat softened as succeeding generations planted their own roots in the soil of Hawaii. Children of missionary families intermarried with the native Hawaiians until they ceased to think of themselves as being on an extended leave from their home base in America: They began to think of themselves as Hawaiians.

And so would the other immigrants, the laborers from the Orient who came to the Islands to work on the sugar plantations. They came from Japan and China, Korea and the Philippines. In the scented evenings, the Asians turned their faces away from their former lands and began to assimilate, to become a part of the Hawaiian milieu. They, like the missionaries, intermarried, and over the decades there grew the particular tolerance

Above, ancestors are remembered with fondness and reverence in this Japanese cemetery in Hamakua.

Opposite, a fisherman seizes a quiet moment in a waterfall of nets.

for other races and other customs that characterizes the Hawaiian Islands today.

Many other changes, not all of them good, lay before the emerging Hawaiians. The Kamehameha dynasty died out and in 1893 the monarchy itself ended in controversy as Hawaii became a republic under control of pro-annexationists. In 1900 organic legislation made Hawaii a Territory of the United States. There had been an evolution of commerce: Sugar replaced whaling, pineapple became a viable industry, and tourism was just over the horizon. The native Hawaiians, who had been reduced by Western diseases from at least 300,000 to less than a third of that number, found themselves at the bottom of the socio-economic ladder and had to fight to regain lost ground.

Through these changes, the economic and political leadership of the Islands had a decidedly conservative cast, lying primarily in the hands of the *haoles*. The *haole* regimes continued through the decades until, on a balmy

Sunday morning in 1941, a Japanese attack on Pearl Harbor plunged America into war.

Hawaii became a staging and refueling base, and a training center. Thousands of Americans were in and out of the Islands en route to war zones. The Islands themselves contributed their share of young men and women, including one group of note: the Japanese-Americans. They fought to get into the U.S. Army to prove their loyalty and, when finally admitted, they fought the enemy with such valor their unit became the most decorated in the American army. After World War II, many of these same ex-infantrymen, firmly grasping law degrees and with their eyes to the future, went into politics. In 1954 they brought about a wholesale defeat of the establishment, opening doors to more liberal ideas—and to all races.

Hawaii's admission as the 50th state of the Union on August 21, 1959, was an occasion of celebration in the Islands, but there were also many whose thoughts went back to the past: to Islands that were independent, and, in an even earlier time, Islands that were uniquely *Hawaiian*.

Much had changed; the Islands no longer were isolated, no matter how geographically remote they might seem. The jet engine and satellite communications brought Hawaii into daily contact with the rest of the world and, for better or worse, there was no turning back. Subject to the same economic vagaries and the same political tides as the rest of the United States, the Hawaiian Islands would evermore move in concert with the other 49 states.

Throughout this dramatic and sometimes turbulent history, the island of Hawaii made significant and lasting contributions. Larger than all the other Hawaiian Islands combined, it was also the most varied. The island contributed thousands of acres for sugar cane, and provided, at Hilo, the second-best deep-water harbor in the archipelago. Volcanoes launched spectacular (and safe) eruptions that added new acreage and drew visitors. The island that produced Kamehameha I, first and most energetic of the monarchs, later produced vigorous legislators who exercised great influence in Territorial and state legislatures. Vast tracts of macadamia nut farms became an economic boon to the island and the state, as did the smooth waters off Kailua-Kona, where giant marlin challenged fishermen from all over the world. Coffee beans grown on the southern slopes of the world's largest shield volcano, Mauna Loa, were rich and tasty; Kona coffee became prized on world markets. On top of the tallest mountain in the Pacific, Mauna

Opposite, some of the island's charm is evident on a Puna road in the soft morning.

Above, the old Hawaiian songs are charming as well, and an important part of Hawaii's rich legacy.

The beautiful black sand beach at Kalapana, at the southeastern edge of Mauna Loa's volcanic flows.

Kea (13,796 feet), observatories sprang up. Telescopes were trained on the strange constellations that the Polynesians had observed on their unprecedented northern voyage of discovery. Splendid resort hotels rose from the dark lava fields along the shorelines, inviting visitors to discover the unmistakable aura of a more distant place and a more gracious time.

Hawaiians are interested in past and present; they are not given to conjecture at length about the future. A fascinating history and heritage have shaped local people in certain ways and the future will offer—whatever it has to offer. The people who live on the island of Hawaii share something more profound, perhaps, than a concern about the future: They share an affinity for the space and soil of their uncommon home. In this respect they echo the *aloha aina,* love for the land, that lay dormant in the hearts of the Polynesians pushing their long canoes past the limits of fear toward a final, welcome landfall.

Path of the Winds

The wind—the Hawaiians call it *moa'e*—is born in the northeast and hurtles across the open ocean to reach the Big Island; it pushes clouds up against the slopes of the volcanoes, gets funneled across the lush uplands of Waimea, and eddies gently around the tropical landscape of Kona. This northeast trade wind brought sailing ships to Hawaii in an earlier time, and today it cools the island and contributes to a climate that causes days to glitter and nights to lie softly on the land and the surrounding sea.

It is a large land, by comparison. Its 4,038 square miles is nearly twice the size of all the other inhabited Hawaiian Islands combined. The very stuff of its creation is on all sides—the porous lava coughed up by five massive volcanoes. The volcanoes themselves dominate the landscape: Mauna Kea (The White Mountain, named for its snowfalls) at 13,796 feet is the highest summit in the state; Mauna Loa (The Long Mountain) is the largest single mountain mass in the world; Hualalai, at 8,271 feet, helps block the *moa'e* and gives the Kona side of the island much of its soft charm; Kohala, at 5,480 feet, presides over some of the most beautiful upland meadows to be found anywhere; and Kilauea Caldera, at 4,090 feet, is one of the most-photographed volcanoes in the world because its peaceful eruptions draw visitors again and again.

Kilauea and Mauna Loa are still active but not killers—at least, so far. Hawaiian eruptions are of a different sort from the explosive eruptions that take place elsewhere and, while not to be taken lightly, they have caused no loss of life in recent times. Damage is another story, as attested to by farmers who have seen their orchids, papayas and anthurium fields buried in crinkly *aa* or fast-flowing *pahoehoe* lava. One

The Hawaiian Islands are the tops of mighty volcanoes, which today still show their awesome power on the Big Island. The result is spectacular landscaping (overleaf) with moments of understated beauty (overleaf inset).

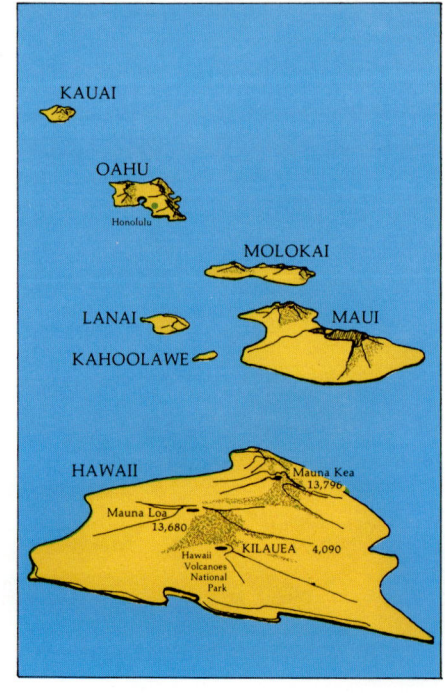

A stroll on a country road has its own rewards: clean air, sunshine, and perhaps a waiting cup of tea.

Opposite, Kamehameha I fought a major battle offshore of this coastline at Waipio Valley.

eruption, in 1960, flattened the village of Kapoho and built a 400-foot hill in the center of what had been a papaya grove.

More devastating than the volcanoes have been the *tsunamis,* misnamed as tidal waves, which race across the ocean as the result of earthquakes and slam up against the Big Island's coast. One of the most devastating occurred on April 1, 1946, as the result of an earthquake in the Aleutian Islands. A 55-foot wall of water crashed into the Big Island's principal city, Hilo, and other areas along the shoreline, killing 159 persons and causing $26 million in damages. Fourteen years later an earthquake in Chile sent a 35-foot wave again into Hilo, killing 61 persons and causing $23 million in damages. Each time the hardy people of Hilo clean up, rebuild, and go about their business, but now a much more sophisticated *tsunami* early warning system reaches across the Pacific Basin to give them warning.

The wind that pushes across the island touches on districts that have distinctive characteristics and styles, and which give the island its great variety. In the area around Hilo on the eastern coast, the ambiance is that of a sleepy little town surrounded by sugar cane and various other crops and flowers, all washed by the Islands' heaviest rainfall. South of Hilo, in the Puna region, the atmosphere is definitely rural "Old Hawaii"; Hawaiian legends and ghost stories abound in the rain forests and lava coastal regions. To the north, in the Waimea-Kohala area, green meadows and Hawaiian cowboys often remind American visitors of Wyoming or Montana, while along the Kona coast there is a certain softness in the air, a very tropical look and feeling. Nothing, however, seems soft about the world of the high volcanoes. The saddle between the two giants, Mauna Kea and Mauna Loa, is a wild region of wind-driven ash cut by a ribbon of road that crests at 6,000 feet, while the mountains rise around it in great dignity. Lava forms of strange shapes, wild goats and occasional flashing pheasants break the monochromatic landscape and then, after a while, the very bleakness of this lonely region takes on a kind of grandeur. On the other side of Mauna Loa, the Kilauea volcano region is less inhospitable, but still presents a "mountains-of-the-moon" appearance. It served, fittingly enough, as a training

site for moon-destined astronauts.

As the land varies, so does the temperature. In a lowland area the temperature may float between 70 and 76 degrees, then drop 20 degrees lower with altitude. The air changes more in the course of a drive from the bottom of a mountain to near the top than it does from winter to summer. Variety is again evident in the physical attractions of the island. Rainbow Falls, in Hilo, is aptly named for the rainbows that break over falls wide but not spectacularly high, while a few miles away on the drive toward Hamakua, Akaka Falls sends a rush of water dropping 442 feet, the longest waterfall in the state. The second-longest water feature in the state also is on the Big Island: The Wailuku River stretches for 32 miles and discharges 184 million gallons of water per day.

As much as any other factor, it is the variety of the people that gives the Big Island its diversified charm. When Captain Cook arrived on the island in 1778-1779, there was an estimated population of 150,000 Hawaiians living there, some 40 percent of the total population of the entire archipelago. The Big Island continued to contain the largest population for the next century, but wars and diseases took their toll, and in 1872 there were only 16,000 people on the island. Shortly afterwards the population increased, but only marginally by Hawaiians. The growth of the sugar industry necessitated the bringing in of laborers from Portugal, China, Japan, Puerto Rico, Spain, Korea and the Philippines; then the population remained steady until mechanization of the sugar industry caused a drop between 1930 and 1960. Recent years have seen a growth in the statistics, and today the island contains some 100,000 people—still fewer than when Captain Cook anchored in Kealakekua Bay on the Kona coast. There is no ethnic majority. Japanese make up some 38 percent of the population, Caucasians about 29 percent, Filipinos about 17 percent, Hawaiians 12 percent, Chinese almost three percent, and others one to two percent. At 22.6 persons per square mile the island has one of the lowest population densities in the state, and the blissful uncrowding contributes to a distinctive Big Island lifestyle. Another contribution is the combined folklore of the various ethnic groups, a folklore which goes through a subtle but definite refining process and comes out—still ethnic, but also Hawaiian. Big Islanders like to feel they have taken the best that each group has to offer and watched it evolve into something very much a part of their own time and place.

Scattered in the path of the wind are

Skill, training—and intensity—go into the production of a successful hula, an Island art form now making a comeback after some years of neglect (opposite).

Above, at Napo'opo'o, a small church is the focus of faith in a land which has known the worship of many gods.

Below, on Hilo Bay, the hotels of Banyan Drive cling to the land but look to the sea. Bottom, early settlers left a kind of sublime graffitti in the form of petroglyphs, rock carvings that were symbolic and artistic.

evidences of man's reach for spiritual understanding. On the island are several important *heiaus,* places of worship for the ancient Hawaiians; the *heiaus* are impressive structures of rock, easily symbolizing the closeness of the Hawaiians to their physical environment. Late-coming religions, brought by dedicated Protestant missionaries and Catholic priests, left their symbols as well: From the incredibly painted St. Benedict's at Honaunau to small, tin-roofed, one-room structures almost fragile in their appearance, they reflect a community's faith and dreams.

Other structures reflect other aims, and again variety is the operative word. Dramatic glass and concrete hotels rise on some excellent beaches; one region of the island is replete with drinking troughs for cattle and horses; another section is dotted with elaborate greenhouses containing hundreds of thousands of flowers; yet another section contains the rickety wooden buildings once used as plantation bunkhouses for Asian laborers who worked their way out of the fields and went on to add their rich backgrounds to the social tapestry of the island.

It is an island where men become very chauvinistic very quickly about their chosen place. The *paniolo,* the Hawaiian cowboy, would never dream of leaving his rolling countryside for what he would consider the steamy atmosphere of Kailua-Kona, while the Kona man, enamoured of the ocean, would never exchange his seaside home for the wet uplands. The easy pace of Hilo is very attractive to men who tend to ignore the heavier rainfall and regard Kona as too dry and warm. To a man, they extol the pleasures of the Big Island when talking to strangers, but each may be talking about his own vision of what the Big Island is.

The Flowered Way

Hilo on a lazy afternoon: A light rain is falling over this sleepy, sugar cane town and the traffic is desultory, as it is at most times, but the golfers are out in spite of the damp. A tour bus heads up toward the volcanoes area—Hilo is the gateway—while other visitors move around and look at the flowers; Hilo is considered one of the world's great flower growing areas. The 140 inches of rainfall a year contribute a watery blessing to fertile soil, and gentle temperatures protect the delicate petals. Orchid and anthurium nurseries abound, throwing bright splashes of color onto a landscape already colorful with an astonishing variety of greenery.

The rain is reaching down into the Puna section of the island, a section that sees long stretches of sugar cane give way to tropical rain forests, the forests stopping abruptly near the edge of sheer black lava cliffs with the sea gnawing at their feet. By day the residents of Puna go about their tasks in the cane fields or papaya groves or flower nurseries, and by night they listen to old Hawaiian tales. It is the proper setting for legends. At night the owls, *pueos,* sit in the low branches of trees along the back roads, and a great yellow moon makes strange shadows of the twisted trees and tall ferns, while an onshore breeze hums in the desolate lava fields below the site of a destroyed town, sending up a melancholy and otherworldly sound.

Nowhere else are the orchids so colorful—or plentiful.

In the other direction from Hilo, on the drive that winds around the eastern coast to the town of Hamakua, great arcing curves in the road mean grand views for motorists, whether facing inward toward the waterfalls and dense foliage or outward toward the long sweep of the sea. Fields of sugar cane stretch away on all sides, accentuated by the presence here and there of the mills and the towns that grew up around them, replete with the small churches, the charming schools, the large houses of the plantation managers, and the comfortable, old-shoe feeling of a place where the residents all know each other. The highway is littered with pieces of cane dropped from the toiling sugar cane trucks, but since sugar is the lifeblood of the region, there are no complaints.

In Hilo itself the rain seldom dampens spirits among the residents, who tend to ignore anything less than a deluge and even then are not easily alarmed. Behind the false-front storefronts, commerce goes on as usual. Schools usually have covered walkways because of the rainfall, but the children are high-spirited. In government offices talk of rain is often discouraged because it could tend to frighten away visitors, but everyone knows the rain makes the flowers and the flowers have been the making of Hilo in recent years.

The town has, of course, many sunny days

Above, quaint buildings and modern enterprises meld easily in Hilo.

Opposite, Hilo's sunny days take on a unique softness that belie the myth, "it always rains in Hilo."

and they are apt to be sparkling. The freshness of the mornings lures people outdoors to taste the air, which sometimes has a salty tang from the crescent bay the town curves around. Down at one end of the bay the pungent smell of fresh fish mingles with the morning and evening airs as fishermen sell their catch. In the distance looms the impressive bulk of Mauna Kea, sometimes etched vividly against a cerulean sky and at other times wearing clouds at the summit. Mauna Loa also is visible occasionally, but it is Mauna Kea that dominates the horizon.

Hilo is a town for strolling. Near the center of the visitor industry, the hotel strip along Banyan Drive, is a park that symbolizes the closeness of Japanese and Hawaiian cultures on this island. Liliuokalani Gardens is splendid with pagodas, stone lanterns, small ponds, brilliantly hued grasses and trees which represent both Japan and Hawaii. The garden was named for Hawaii's last queen, but designed by a Japanese landscape artist. It is inviting and well kept. Equally inviting is a stroll "downtown," where the facades of the stores are pastels under tin roofs, creating a sense of timelessness. It is obvious that Hilo residents like their town the way it is.

Some attractions—In Hilo:

Liliuokalani Gardens, off Banyan Drive, is a thirty-acre representation of the best of Japanese landscaping, with a Hawaiian flavor, good for strolling, picnicking, or just sitting.

Sampan Harbor on Lihiwai Street between Banyan Drive and Liliuokalani Gardens is a place where fishermen sell their catch, usually before breakfast and at *pau hana*, the end of the work day, around 4 p.m.

Haili Church at 404 Haili Street is where

Opposite, upper left, Akaka Falls, celebrated in song and story, is the state's longest waterfall and a major visitor attraction. Lower left, even small streams become impressive in the midst of an artistic grove of bamboo. Above, the hardy anthurium has become a staple of the Island flower industry.

you can hear services in both Hawaiian and English. Built by Protestant missionaries in 1859, the church is reminiscent of New England.

Lyman Mission House & Museum at 276 Haili Street was built in 1839 by missionaries and is a walk back in time. It was built with timbers hewed from local forests and with coral mortaring. The museum shows tools and artifacts from early Hawaii as well as displays depicting the local environment and man's use of it.

Rainbow Falls, on the Wailuku River, is a refreshing pause where rainbows highlight the morning spray from the falls; nearby is a picnic area.

Ke Kilohana O Ka Malamalama at 558 Manono Street is a charming shoe box of a church with Victorian touches, where you can hear services in English and Hawaiian. It is a Protestant church, noted for its choirs and its Hawaiian language classes.

Fifteen miles north of Hilo on Route 19 there is a four-mile cutoff that leads to a wild grotto of bamboo, gardenias, orchids and fern, all cut by an easy path that leads to a lookout where you can sit and view a magnificent plunge of water. **Akaka Falls** drops more than 400 feet from the point where it pitches over a precipice to the point where spray boils up from Kolekole Stream, far below. If you are lucky you will see a Hawaiian hawk, *Io*, hunting above the falls, hanging almost motionless on the soft currents until it makes its sudden, flashing dive.

—In Puna:

In the small town of **Pahoa**, 19 miles south of Hilo, you can see a number of anthurium nurseries blossoming side by side with fruit trees and palms. This sleepy town is more or less the slow heartbeat of the Puna District and is pleasant to wander through.

Liliuokalani Gardens offers quiet repose and interesting walks in an Oriental setting. Opposite, the ambiance of a quiet country town is both pervasive and peaceful.

Hilo's Rainbow Falls, in wet and dry seasons, shows its different moods (above). Right, in any season, the harbor of Suisan fish market attracts buyers of fish fresh from the ocean depths.

Three miles east of Pahoa on Route 132 is **Lava Tree State Park**, certainly worth spending some time in. Here, on its way to the sea, the lava engulfed the trees in its path before they burned, leaving chimneylike lava sculptures as it cooled.

Another worthwhile visit is to the abandoned **lighthouse at Cape Kumukahi**, where Route 132 stops at the edge of the land. In 1960 a lava flow threatened the entire area but the lighthouse keeper kept insisting that Pele, the Fire Goddess, would not destroy his light. He was right; the light remained untouched by the lava which surrounded it a few feet away. The lava effectively put the light out of commission, however, by destroying the six or seven structures that supported it. Today the light is inoperative, a curious survivor of one of the more spectacular eruptions in Hawaii's recent volcanic history.

From Cape Kumukahi, or from Pahoa, it is an interesting drive to **Kalapana**, site of a black sand beach and a favorite area for photographers. Here you will find a small, clean beach park and the remains of the **Kekaloa Heiau**. Worth looking into is the nearby **Star of the Sea Church**, with its fascinating interior of mosaics, and just behind the church are the enormous stone slabs from which ancient Hawaiians launched their outrigger canoes.

A few miles farther down the road is **Queen's Bath**, a natural swimming hole frequented by youngsters, and a couple of miles beyond that is the entrance to the Kalapana section of the **Hawaii Volcanoes National Park**. There is a visitor center, a hiking trail through a scenic park, and picnic and campground areas. There is also the remains of **Wahaula Heiau** ("The Red Mouth"), 700 years old and site of the last human sacrifices in the Islands. It was twice rebuilt and was one of a handful of *luakini heiaus*, places of worship for the kingdom's *alii*, or chieftains.

On the road between Kalapana and Cape Kumukahi, Route 137, lies **Mackenzie State Park**, a cliffside haven where the wind rustles through pine trees and the ocean pounds the rocks on the shoreline below. The park is a fine place for picnicking or for simply sitting and listening to the natural sounds of wind, waves, birds and the chattering of mongooses in the brush.

Hilo and its environs usually are touted in guide books as the jumping off point for other parts of the island. This is a true but inadequate description, for Hilo, the Akaka Falls, Puna and Kapalana areas are worth more than a cursory look. To appreciate this interesting district requires a little time and effort, a willingness to explore and learn, and a dedication to a more leisurely interfacing with its people and places.

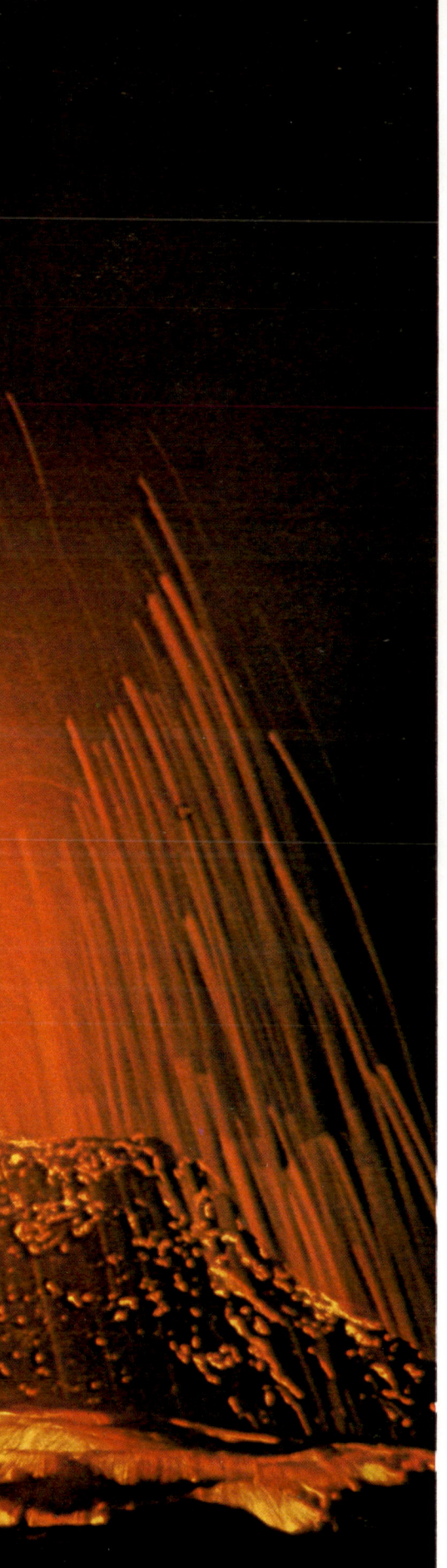

Goddess of Snow, Goddess of Fire

In the high world of the volcanoes there is a moment when the strange calm of the morning begins to give way, and the air starts to crackle; light bounces from the distant sea and the wind begins to rise. Until then the stillness that has lain across the mountains has seemed complete and unbreakable, as if no one dared intrude on the sleep of the goddesses. But then the morning stirs with a bird call, and the harmonics of the wind through the trees at the timberline call visitors out to smell the freshness, to taste the air.

Residents and visitors alike will note the shifting moods of the volcanoes area: the sudden rains, the incredibly sparkling mornings, the sense of well-being when the sun falls golden over the lava fields and sends spears of light down into the thick forests of fern and ohia. Everywhere there is a feeling of being present among elemental forces; at every turn there is a vista and a sense of space, while underfoot is the very matter of earth, the omnipresent lava, the building material of the island.

Five volcanoes sculpted the island—Mauna Kea, Mauna Loa, Kilauea, Hualalai and Kohala—but it is Mauna Loa and Kilauea that most visitors explore, for reasons of convenience. Kilauea is one of the world's most active volcanoes and draws sightseers even when quiet, for its fantastic landscape—its back-of-the-moon appearance—is interesting and pleasing and changing with every transformation of the weather.

A Mauna Ulu spatter cone tosses cooling lava in this time exposure of the lava's trajectories.

The incredible fecundity of basaltic soil produces a richness of growing plants.

In 1916 a national park was established at Kilauea to preserve its natural beauties and its rare birds and plant life. Parts of Mauna Loa were included, along with a section of Puna coastline, to give the park an area of 344 square miles. Visitors who want to see as much as possible of the park, safely, begin with a trip to the park's visitor center near the Kilauea Caldera. This crater measures 2.5 miles by 2 miles by some 400 feet deep at the summit, and contains Halemaumau, a firepit which some believe is the home of the goddess of fire, Pele. Around Kilauea's summit is a network of trails that range from easy walks through a bizarre landscape to strenuous hikes to the summit of Mauna Loa. Each has its rewards.

When Kilauea erupts it may be contained in Halemaumau, or it may be a flank eruption, occurring somewhere else in the caldera itself or outside it in the surrounding forest areas or in the lava desert site of earlier eruptions. Kilauea's eruptions in the past 30 years have been numerous and varied, ranging from small "spatter cones" to towering fire fountains nearly 2,000 feet high. The eruptions, however, are usually gentle in comparison with those elsewhere in the world, so visitors can watch the birth of new land in safety—and in awe. Like nothing else on earth, an eruption reminds us that mankind still dwells on a living planet.

Islanders react to the eruptions by trying to get to the scene as quickly as possible. Some older Hawaiians make offerings to Pele, the tempestuous goddess of fire. Traditionally, these offerings have been gifts of ohelo berries, the sweet red berries that grow in the volcanoes area, but in recent years the gift may include a bottle of gin left in the path of an advancing lava flow. The gifts are to ensure that Pele does not kill or destroy.

The Pele legends are strong and pervasive in the volcanoes region, and have obscured the fact that the area is occupied by more than one goddess. In the mythology of the Hawaiians there were four maidens with white mantles, all beautiful, witty, fun-loving and adventurous—and none of them friendly with Pele. These snow goddesses were Poliahu, who lived on

Left, deliberate underexposure shows the volcano's structure: a hot, orange interior and darker shades of cooling lava.

Fast flows often produce the ropy pahoehoe lava (top, right) and in time the old flows again support life (above).

Mauna Kea; Lilinoe, the goddess of Haleakala volcano on Maui; Waiau, who also lived on Mauna Kea; and Kahoupokane, the goddess of the volcano Hualalai. The latter three are obscure indeed, and Poliahu has almost passed from memory. But it was Poliahu who battled Pele to the uneasy truce that exists in the volcanoes area today. That two beautiful women would be rivals may not be surprising, but the intensity of that rivalry led to earth-shaking action:

> "Pele... called for the forces of fire to burst open the doors of the subterranean caverns of Mauna Kea. Up toward the mountain she marshalled her fire-fountains. Poliahu fled toward the summit. The snow-mantle was seized by the outbursting lava and began to burn up. Poliahu grasped the robe, dragging it away and carrying it with her. Soon she regained her strength and threw the mantle over the mountains. There were earthquakes upon earthquakes, shaking the great Island from sea to sea."*

As the battle continued the lava streams were beaten back, checked and chilled. The lava ran, the snow fell and the island was shaken to its core. Finally, it was over, and while Pele was occupying the lower half of the volcanoes, Poliahu reigned supreme at the summits. The old Hawaiians believed Poliahu always would be victorious, but they maintained their healthy respect for Pele's powers and her temper.

Some attractions—At the Summit:

A 3.2-mile trail starts near the door of **Volcano House**, a rustic and charming hotel on the rim of the crater, and crosses the strange landscape of the crater itself to **Halemaumau firepit**. The trail is conveniently marked and is popular with many visitors.

Other trails lead out into the Ka'u desert of lava where you can see the footprints of an army that was caught in a sudden eruption in 1790. Most of the footprints have been eroded, but they are reminders that the eruptions are not to be taken too lightly. Another trail stretches across a half-mile of cinders that fell from the Kilauea Iki (Little Kilauea) eruption of late 1959. Called **Devastation Trail**, the boardwalk winds through stark, stripped trees that fell victim to the plummeting ash. Much of the foliage has reappeared but the starkness of the cinders area provides a study in contrasts.

Pele and the Snow Goddess, Hawaiian Legends of Volcanoes, by W.D. Westervelt, Charles E. Tuttle Company, Rutland, Vt, and Tokyo.

Opposite, a fire fountain in full fury pumps out lava, measured in cubic yards, that builds the island.

Above, geologist Wayne Ault, in heat-reflecting suit, collects lava samples from Kilauea Iki. The samples give clues as to the source area of the lava.

Fire and water collide as lava pours into the ocean along the Kealakomo seashore.

One quarter-mile trail leads through a forest where giant ferns and other trees grow beside a variety of native Hawaiian plants, marked by identifying signs. A wide variety of birds live in the fern forest and their calls alone would be worth the walk. But this trail also leads to the **Thurston Lava Tube**, a 450-foot tunnel 6 to 20 feet high formed when the outer crust of lava cooled, allowing the molten magma inside to continue to flow. From its formation in prehistoric times to the present, the lava tube has remained empty. Today it is both an oddity and evidence of the incalculable power of fast-flowing lava.

Not unlike the short hike through the fern forest, **Bird Park** (Kipuka Puaulu) is a nature hike trailing off the Mauna Loa strip road which intersects with Route 11, the Hilo-to-Kona highway. Here in microcosm are many of Hawaii's native hardwoods, identified by markers. The trees are homes for a variety of bird life that provides musical accompaniment to hikers making the mile-long loop. On quiet mornings in Bird Park, and most of them are quiet, visitors sometimes hear wild pigs in the underbrush.

All around the summit there are overlooks that present fine views of **Kilauea Caldera**. Brooding behind Kilauea is **Mauna Loa**, sometimes showing snow at its summit; the landscape of this enormous volcano changes with the time of day, the passing clouds and the angle of the sun.

The **Mauna Loa trail**, in contrast to many of the trails around Kilauea, is not for novices. It is a grueling overnight hike to a cabin at 10,000 feet and then on to the summit and back. It must be planned carefully to avoid accidents or injuries in a remote area where help is not easily found. Hikers should notify the park's rangers before setting off. But once on the mountain, a world opens up above the clouds, and the barren landscape assumes an ethereal beauty. In the distance the horizon begins to curve; one feels a sense of wonder and a strange peace. In this atmosphere it is remarkably easy to accept the idea that goddesses of snow and fire live here.

—Adjacent Areas:

From the summit of Kilauea, Route 11 drops into the **Ka'u** area, the southwestern slope of the volcano. It is a region regarded by many as barren and stark, but to those who appreciate the beauty of desolate places, the area is rich and pleasing to the eye. Winter rains bring the area alive with bushes of *alahe'e,* bearing small, white blossoms with a sweet smell.

Volcanic gases form a basaltic bubble (top left) and burn brightly in the Ka'u Desert area (center). Escaping fumes leave crystals of yellow sulphur; in time, the volcanic desert could be covered by abundant pili grass such as in this field (above) near Mauna Ulu. This is the home of Pele (facing page), the immortal goddess of volcanoes, shown in contrast with Poliahu, the snow goddess.

Along Route 11 is the small town of **Pahala** with its sugar mill, and behind it a lush valley accessible in the dry season by a cane-haul road. In 1868 a mud slide buried a village here; at the same time there were simultaneous eruptions of Mauna Loa and Kilauea, and a dropping of part of the Puna coastline by more than five feet.

Farther along Route 11 is **Punaluu**, a small settlement which most visitors never see, and a black sand beach which most of them do. To the east of the beach are the ruins of **Kaneeleele Heiau**. Not far away are the ruins of two other ancient temples.

The road leads to, but does not end at, **South Point**. On this wind-battered cape the Polynesian voyagers may have made their first footprints in the Islands. Remnants of the oldest-known settlement, dating from 750 A.D., were discovered here.

From Ka Lae (South Point), the southernmost part of the United States, the road turns north again and continues up the leeward side of the island. Visitors enter the beginning of the Kona area and suddenly find there is still another mood to this amazing island.

But the volcanoes are hard to forget. In that high, crisp world of fire and snow, of warring goddesses and striking contrasts, there is a magical charm and an intoxicating sense of well-being. Different in fact and in mood from the rest of Hawaii, the volcanoes area sings its own siren song that is, for many, truly irresistible.

The Whispering Sea

*E*very man's dream of the South Seas begins to take shape here in this milieu that blends boats, green hillsides, lush tropical foliage, a slower pace and an instant, unmistakable air of *laissez faire*. The waves break on the shore so gently their sound is subdued and caressing, giving rise to the concept of the whispering sea. In Kona the sun is at its best, both rising and setting, and the soft and balmy airs of the seacoast begin to work their strange magic until problems are postponed and soon forgotten.

There is a tropical flavor in Kona despite its modern buildings and occasional traffic accidents. Nothing intrudes on the serenity of the sea. Behind the town of Kailua-Kona, the center of activity in this 60-mile area, Hualalai volcano rises majestically; beyond that is the giant, Mauna Loa. Both volcanoes deflect the wind and give Kona its ambiance of stillness and peace. The wind eventually forms up again out to sea, but in the lee of the volcanoes the Kona area knows an enormous calm.

With Kona's charms and beguiling manners, it is all too easy to overlook its historical importance. On the north side of the Kailua-Kona pier is Kamakahonu beach and small lagoon, where Kamehameha I had a residence; it is here he died in 1819. In keeping with his stature as the greatest of the *alii* (the rulers), his bones were hidden away and remain so to this day. In the center of Kailua-Kona stands Hulihee Palace, a structure of great charm, built in 1837 by Kuakini, brother of Kamehameha's favorite wife, Kaahumanu. Later it served as the summer palace for another king, Kalakaua, and is now an interesting museum. Across the street from the palace is the oldest church in the Islands, Mokuaikaua, also built in 1837. Constructed by missionaries of ohia trees, coral and rock, the church reflects the solid dedication of its builders. At nearby Keauhou Bay is a marker noting the birthplace of still another king, Kamehameha III.

Another marker is found farther down the coast at Kealakekua Bay. It is a single white

Time passes slowly in Milolii, a fishing village on the Kona Coast noted for its sunny, easy ways. Milolii residents are accustomed to visiting artists and photographers, but the village remains unspoiled and remote with an off-the-beaten-path charm.

Built by the brother-in-law of one king, Kamehameha I, Hulihee Palace served as the summer home of a later one, Kalakaua (top). The obelisk (above) marks the site where Capt. Cook died. Cook, already famous when he discovered Hawaii for the West, named the Islands for his patron, the Earl of Sandwich.

obelisk showing the spot where Captain James Cook, who discovered Hawaii for the Western world, was killed in a melee with the Hawaiians in 1779. The obelisk stands across the bay from Hikiau Heiau, the temple where Cook was honored in a special ceremony not long before his death. There he made the tragic mistake of allowing the Hawaiians to believe he was their god Lono. His death followed shortly after it was revealed that Cook was only human, after all.

Hikiau Heiau bears a plaque honoring Henry Opukahaia, whose tales of Hawaii in far-off America fired Protestant missionaries with a zeal to come to the Islands. It was, in fact, in the Kona area that the missionaries made their first landfall and began the work that changed the course of Hawaii's history.

South of Captain Cook lies one of the most-visited historical sites in the Hawaiian Islands, the *pu'uhonua* (place of refuge) at Honaunau, a national historical park. In ancient Hawaii the site was a haven for lawbreakers, or for warriors who were vanquished in battle, fleeing from a relentless enemy. Although there were more than one of such sanctuaries in Old Hawaii, the one at Honaunau is linked to the Kamehameha dynasty and is the most important and best preserved.

Pu'uhonua O Honaunau was an active sanctuary for at least 400 years. During that time, escaping convicts or defeated warriors would defy the odds posed by their pursuers, time, distance, and their own endurance to get inside its high walls and undergo a ceremony of purification. When it was finished they were considered cleansed by the ancient gods, their rulers and the *kahuna*, or priest, who conducted them through the ritual. Cloaked in this protection, the man could then return free to his home and take his place in society without fear.

Today the sanctuary is an interesting and pleasant place where trees, a lava coastline and a gentle breeze invite lazing in the sun. That the sanctuary is here at all is something of a miracle: In 1829 the *kapu* system (the rigid taboos that defined conduct) was overthrown, which resulted in the destruction of the old gods and old traditions. Much of the temple site was razed. The temple's foundations and the lengthy wall around the sanctuary escaped serious damage and in time became the center of restoration efforts. New images of the old gods were carved and, in 1961, when the site became a national park, the area was on its way to recovery. Improvements on the site continue today.

Wooden images are dominant features of Puʻuhonua O Honaunau, a sanctuary for some 400 years. Today it is a place where old skills and crafts, such as the making of fish nets, are preserved.

Coffee is an aromatic industry of the Kona region, which produces gourmet brews.

Throughout the Kona region there is not only a sense of history but a feeling that the present is important, too. The residents of Kona do not march to a different drummer—they move languidly to a music that is part natural sounds of wind and water, and part what they have created. The Kona ambiance is a melding of nature and creature comforts, of naturalness and hedonism. The day's hard work on a charter fishing boat eases into an evening of candlelit dinners and good wines. A sweaty day on a Kona coffee farm ends in a quiet time on a *lanai*, sipping a cold drink and watching the lights come on in the village. There is both a great concentration on taking care of the visitors, a leading industry, and letting the visitors go their own way. Residents are inclined to be helpful but not pushy; visitors are inclined to find Kona people friendly but very much involved in their own affairs.

Some attractions—In Kailua-Kona:

Kailua and its nearby neighbor, **Keauhou Bay**, is the center for fine dining and shopping. Dramatic hotels provide all the amenities, and a stroll down **Alii Drive** in the heart of Kailua is a prerequisite to the evening meal. Fishermen on the seawall in Kailua range widely in ages but are one in the spirit of the moment. Offshore, the calm waters invite sunset cruises and dinner sails on the smoothest waters to be found in the Islands.

Fisher-folk on the sea wall in Kailua-Kona (opposite page) care less for style and more for savoring the moment. Above, a big one that did not get away is weighed on the pier at Kailua-Kona, focal point of an annual tourney that draws fishing teams from all over the world.

Kailua has deservedly become the center of world billfishing competition. Teams from all over the world congregate here to go after record marlin, and get them. This Super Bowl of sport fishing has made Kona famous. On the pier in Kailua the fish are photographed and weighed and as the tournament continues the competition heightens.

From Kailua to Keauhou, the roads ramble through *kiawe* groves and an ever-increasing number of houses. Alii Drive rolls by **White Sands Beach**, a popular swimming area, and **Kahaluu Beach Park**, an excellent place for swimming and picnicking adjacent to a hotel whose grounds hold remains of two ancient heiaus.

—The Countryside:

Above Kailua and reaching down to the vicinity of the **Place of Refuge**, the cooler climate of the volcanic slopes lends itself to the coffee farms which have made Kona coffee a gourmet's delight around the world. Coffee trees grow to the edge of the highway in some

areas and a good cup of Kona coffee ends most meals in this part of the Big Island.

North of Kailua-Kona the **Queen Kaahumanu Highway** takes autos quickly through lava fields, generally lying as straight as an arrow and making it easy to travel to the northern part of the island. The road has taken away much of the traffic from an older highway farther inland, but there is seldom much traffic anyway. The Queen's Highway leads easily to the two finest beaches on the island: one at **Anaehoomalu**, where new hotels have been built without destroying ancient tide pools in the lava; and the other at **Hapuna**, a great white-sand beach from which swimmers often watch humpback whales playing offshore.

South of Kailua-Kona, through the coffee belt, Routes 18 and 11 meet at **Honalo** with its splendid Buddhist temple, and goes on (as Route 11) to **Kealakekua**, with its churches and banks. Kealakekua is a major center on the Kona coast, but keeps its rural look.

Route 11 continues to Honaunau, a wonderfully painted church named **St. Benedict's**, the ancient sanctuary, and then leads to Milolii directly on the coastline. **Milolii** is a town made up primarily of Hawaiian-Filipinos, a fishing village that kept its antique look and atmosphere long after others had abandoned theirs. Today the village is still remote but reachable; visitors sometimes spend a few hours simply

Macadamia nut orchards (opposite page) produce the exquisite nut considered a delicacy around the world.

Above, the 'Ahu'ena Heiau is a reconstruction of a temple used by the first ruler of all the Hawaiian Islands, Kamehameha I.

Below, the triathlon is a demanding swim-run-bike event in Kona that has become an international event.

51

sitting in the shade, enjoying the slow pace of this quiet village.

Beyond Milolii the road goes to the small settlement of **Waiohinu** and then to **Naalehu**, another of the sleepy communities that lie like beads on a string down this stretch of the Kona coast. This area is beautiful with macadamia nut trees, cattle ranches and long acres of rolling countryside. It is a gentle land that gives way to cooler climates and changing vegetation as the road climbs up again and heads toward the totally different world of the volcanoes.

The Kona District is one of the most tropical sections of the inhabited Hawaiian Islands. It matches the popular vision of a Pacific island with its swaying palms, clear waters and easy pace. And yet, like the Big Island as a whole, Kona encompasses a variety of scenes and styles from which its residents pick and choose, all the while wondering why anyone would want to live anywhere else.

Tranquility is the mood of the Kona Coast, especially on a good boat in calm waters (opposite). Quiet beaches also reflect the unhurried pace of an area where a slower pace is infectious.

Mist and Mystique

As dusk begins to blur the distances and lights wink on in the town of Kamuela, the great herds of cattle begin to group themselves leisurely, while cowboys gently urge their horses to take them home, and a light mist begins to spread across the hills and meadows. The sun drops in a final flickering of light. Across the distant pasture comes the anxious cry of a calf and the welcoming response from its mother. On the edge of the vast Parker Ranch two wranglers on horseback talk about the branding soon to come, and the new saddle one of them has ordered from a mail-order place in Texas. Their language is rich with Island pidgin, but they are talking cows and horses and rodeos. This is a Hawaii unlike that known by most visitors and many other Islanders—cool, wind-swept, grassland plains, washed by frequent mists and blessed with an absence of urban problems. This is cowboy country, 2,500 miles away from the American West.

A series of small, dark, red-colored streams crossed this region long before the first Europeans came. The native Hawaiians referred to the region as "red water," or Waimea. In time the name came to embrace the entire region from Hamakua to Kawaihae, Mauna Kea and the Kohala mountains. For a time Waimea was a source of strength for Kamehameha I, who drew from the area's relatively dense population for his soldiers. The cattle came in 1793, when a British naval officer, Captain George Vancouver, brought the first cows to the Big Island as part of an attempt to re-establish good relations between Great Britain and Hawaii. (Only 14 years earlier Captain James Cook had been killed at Kealakekua Bay.)

Vancouver brought five cows and a bull, all purchased from Spanish missions in California. When he presented them to Kamehameha, that shrewd chieftain imposed a ten-year *kapu* (taboo) on killing or hurting the animals. Other cattle began to arrive from California to be

Snow-capped Mauna Kea towers over a pastoral scene that delights the eye in a clean, wind-swept region.

The Wyoming or Montana atmosphere often surprises visitors who are expecting only beaches and palm trees.

A wandering stream (facing page) cuts its way through the green grass of Waimea.

Below, fine horses are appreciated by the paniolos—the cowboys—who work the vast ranges in a tradition going back more than a century in Hawaii.

placed under *kapu* as well; Kamehameha wanted to give them time to produce. It was an effective *kapu*: They proliferated. Herds of cattle became common sights, some of them were wild and dangerous. Cattle hunters, active after the death of Kamehameha, risked death and injuries in their profession but seldom tried to tame any of the cattle.

Hawaiians first came in contact with horses due to a growing trade with the Spanish in America; the opportunity for Hawaiians to appreciate fine horses came in 1828 when a ship brought 17 animals from San Diego. Hawaiian government officials quickly made the connection, and, in about 1832, vaqueros from California, Mexico and South America arrived to control the government's herds. Before long Waimea's economy revolved around saddles, bridles and similar items, while Waimea itself took on some aspects of Spanish culture and the look of a cow town of the southwestern United States. Hawaiian cowboys became quite adept at learning from the vaqueros, whom they called "paniolos," Hawai-

This cowboy's home on the range is not Kansas but Kamuela; dress and lifestyles are very much alike.

ian for Spanish. Corrals and cattle pens, troughs and stables became part of Waimea's culture.

The vast holdings of today's Parker Ranch began with John Palmer Parker, a New England sailor who sought his fortunes in Hawaii and found them. He married a Hawaiian girl, Kipikane, and homesteaded on a small tract of land given him by Kamehameha. Parker became a famous cattle hunter and trader, providing beef to ships replenishing in Hawaii. He was granted two acres of land on the Waimea plains and made them the nucleus of his ranching operations, which decades later had expanded to some 300,000 acres.

As with everything else, ranching in Hawaii took on subtle Hawaiian overtones. Cowboys wearing chaps and spurs spoke pidgin, ate Japanese food and strummed Irish songs on ukuleles—stringed instruments from Portugal. The people of Waimea would go to horse races and rodeos, and, only a few days later, to the familiar ocean where they fished and swam. The close connection between these divergent lifestyles and types of recreation was, and is, possible because of the terrain. The town of Kamuela ("Samuel," in Hawaiian, named for a later Parker) is the heart of the Waimea cattle region and lies 2,400 feet above sea level, but is only 10 miles up from a splendid beach park and the nearby boat harbor of Kawaihae.

On the other side of the Kohala mountains lie small towns with euphonious names: Hawi, Kapaau, Niulii. It is a marvelous place for history. Kamehameha I was born in this region; a statue of him stands proudly at Kapaau. Near Kapaau is an enormous boulder said to

A statue of Kamehameha I near Hawi is a visitor attraction (left).

North from Kamuela, a mountain road offers panoramic vistas (below).

have been carried from the sea to a nearby heiau by Kamehameha, who was noted for his strength.

Between the North Kohala region and Kamuela lie the Kohala mountains, cresting at 3,564 feet. The connecting road is one of the most spectacular drives in the entire Island chain; as Waimea is approached over the mountains, some 40 miles of coastline stretch off in the distance, and in clear view are Mauna Kea, Mauna Loa and Hualalai.

Waimea is growing in popularity as a place where Islanders escape the pace of more urbanized areas. The cattle country is clean, wind-washed, green and scenic. Stately trees serve as windbreaks and houses huddle against the sides of the hills. Rambling wooden fences enclose pastures of sweet-tasting grasses for cattle and horses, and towering behind it all, often brilliant with snow, is Mauna Kea.

Some attractions—In Kamuela:

Parker Ranch Center features a museum and theatre, where you can watch a film presentation of the story of Parker Ranch and view an interesting collection of ranch artifacts.

Imiola Church, built in 1857 by a famous missionary, Lorenzo Lyons, is open to visitors. The church walls are paneled in *koa*, a beautiful Hawaiian hardwood. The choir sings hymns in

For more than a hundred years Imiola Church has been a landmark in Waimea for residents and visitors alike.

59

Hawaiian written a century ago by Lyons.

Kamuela itself is worth a leisurely drive or stroll; it is a large village rather than a metropolis. Many homes have a gingerbread facade, as do some of the businesses. The town is a strange but appealing blend of New England, the American Southwest, and a Pacific island.

—Beyond Kamuela:

On the seashore below Kamuela is **Kawaihae**, a harbor with a small town and a small marina. At this site the first cattle were landed on the island. Later the first horses also were off-loaded here.

Pu'ukohola and **Mailekini heiaus** are south of Kawaihae and easily visited. Pu'ukohola is a massif with a huge rock platform, and was built in 1791 by Kamehameha, who dedicated it to his war god, Kukailimoku. Kamehameha's last rival for power on the Big Island, Keoua, was killed here as he stepped ashore for the heiau's dedication. Across the road, Mailekini Heiau is an older temple once used as a fort.

Mahukona Beach Park is a fine place for swimming, either from the park itself or from

the old landing nearby from which sugar was shipped off the island.

North of Mahukona is another beach park, **Kapaa**, which is one of the finest snorkeling beaches on the island.

Still farther north is **Mookini Heiau**, the first registered national historic landmark in the state and one of the two sacrificial temples of the highest rank, built by the Tahitian priest, Paao, in the 13th century.

Near the end of the road is **Keokea Beach Park**, a scenic seashore good for picnicking but dangerous for swimming.

Kamuela homes tend to be comfortable and warm, reflecting the interesting and unusual blend of Hawaiian and Old West styles that give the area its great charm.

Beyond the beach park the road ends with a view of **Pololu Valley**, broad and green. Beyond Pololu is **Waipio**, a huge valley of historic importance. Waipio is rich with burial caves, and, offshore, Kamehameha fought an important battle using foreign weapons and foreign advisors. Waipio is accessible from **Honokaa**, a small town on the opposite side of the valley.

In Waimea the residents leave their area to go elsewhere with great and understandable reluctance. There is a Waimea style of living that needs those cool uplands to make it all feasible, and those who do venture out of the region hurry back as quickly as possible. It is a style made up of the business of ranching and the pursuit of leisure-time activities centering around horses, mountain trails and plenty of space. Enhancing these pursuits are the sounds —the wind in the eucalyptus trees; the smells— the strong, rich smell of cantering horses, or the comforting smell of wood smoke on a cold evening; and the sights—the close-up charm of Waimea's green grass or the long, unmatched vistas expanding outward to the limit of the eye, but not the heart. To leave Waimea for long periods of time causes a wrench to the soul, but to arrive back again after a long absence is to experience that best of all feelings: It is, simply, to come home.

Each evening the disappearance of the sun into the sea serves as a reminder that the land is dwarfed by the world's mightiest ocean. To be an Islander is to divide the heart—love the sea, love the land.

Aloha Aina

It is probably the secret dream of every artist or writer to know pure vision, to see a thing whole and clean and to see *all* of it—its spiritual and historical sides as well as the physical, and perhaps, to try to see its future. To view the Big Island and try to see it truly is to become aware of a great inadequacy, to come to a realization that there is so much to this spectacular place that it is futile to try to unlock all its doors, to uncover all its secrets.

It seems to me that the Big Island's future lies in how well it remembers its past. Born in violence, raked by conflicting cultures, the island has triumphed because it has kept— more than any other island—a certain mystery in its inner heart. No one can know all the songs the island sings, and no one should. Men have come to the island with different purposes in their hearts—some to plunder, some to preach—but the island worked its secret ways on them until the men began to change rather than the island. If the Big Island continues to cast its particular spell, it will be because men ultimately do not want to change it. It will be because the Island people remain aware of the joys and blessings to be derived from their uncommon home.

The love of the land, *Aloha Aina*, is the gift men can give back to the island. And if in future years men seek a place of refuge, a sanctuary from the problems and cares of the world, it will be there for them as it has always been, an island of fire and snow, coming out of the sea at the end of an epic voyage, rich in promise and cloaked in beauty and mystery; an island of dreams.

CREDITS

Photography

Front and back covers: Brett Uprichard

Title page: Robert B. Goodman

Frontispiece: Allan Seiden

A Note in the Beginning: Brett Uprichard

In the Wake of the Long Canoes
  p. 7, Boone Morrison; pp. 8-12, Brett Uprichard; p. 13, Boone Morrison; p. 14, Brett Uprichard

Path of the Winds
  p. 16, Richard P. Wirtz; p. 17, Mathias Van Hesemans; pp. 18-21, Brett Uprichard; p. 22, Susan Merritt; pp. 23-24, Brett Uprichard

The Flowered Way
  p. 25, Pat Pitzer; pp. 26-31, Brett Uprichard; p. 32, Hawaii Visitors Bureau (black and white); p. 32, Brett Uprichard (color)

Goddess of Snow, Goddess of Fire
  pp. 34-35, Robin T. Holcomb; p. 36, Boone Morrison; p. 37, Robin T. Holcomb (upper left); p. 37, Brett Uprichard (upper right and bottom); p. 38, Robert B. Goodman; p. 39, Donald A. Swanson; pp. 40-41, Richard Grigg; p. 42, Robert I. Tilling (top left); p. 42, Glen Kaye (middle and bottom left); p. 42, Boone Morrison (top right)

The Whispering Sea
  pp. 44-46, Brett Uprichard; p. 47, Douglas Peebles (top right); p. 47, Steven Kastner (inset); p. 47, Brett Uprichard (black and white); p. 48, Allan Seiden (top); p. 48, Brett Uprichard (bottom); p. 49, Douglas Peebles; p. 50, Werner Stoy; p. 51, Pat Pitzer (top); p. 51, Carol Hogan (bottom); p. 52, Brett Uprichard

Mist and Mystique
  pp. 54-57, Brett Uprichard; p. 58, Allan Seiden; pp. 59-61, Brett Uprichard

Aloha Aina
  pp. 62-63, Brett Uprichard

Illustrations

  p. 6: Herb Kane
  p. 8: Franklin Luke
  pp. 15, 24, 33, 43, 53, 62: Linda Leonard

Book Design: Teresa J. Black